North American
River Otters

Other titles in the Returning Wildlife series include:

The Bald Eagle
Bats
The North American Beaver

Returning Wildlife

North American
River Otters

John E. Becker

KIDHAVEN PRESS

THOMSON

———————✦———————
GALE

Detroit • New York • San Diego • San Francisco
Boston • New Haven, Conn. • Waterville, Maine
London • Munich

To my mother, whose encouragement and support made this book possible.

Library of Congress Cataloging-in-Publication Data

Becker, John E., 1942–
  North American river otters / by John E. Becker.
    p. cm. — (Returning wildlife)
  Includes bibliographical references
Summary: Discusses the near extinction, return, and future of
river otters.
  ISBN 0-7377-0755-0 (hardback)
  1. Lontra canadensis—Juvenile literature. 2. Endangered species—
Juvenile literature. [1. Otters. 2. Endangered species.]
I. Title. II. Series.
  QL737.C25 B425 2002
  599.769'2—dc21

2001006272

Contents

chapter 1

Otters Disappear

Otters are some of nature's most playful animals. They love nothing better than to slide down a snowy hillside or splash into the water for a quick swim. Today, people enjoy otters for their playfulness and consider them important animals. Yet, for a long time, many people valued otters only for the money that could be made from trapping them to satisfy the demand for their pelts.

During the nineteenth century, otters were killed for their fur in such great numbers that their once abundant population dropped to low levels. The species was driven closer to **extinction** by water pollution and loss of **wetlands**. By the 1960s, otters were gone from much of the middle portion of America.

In the 1970s, after environmental protection laws forced the cleanup of polluted water, state **wildlife** agencies began "reintroducing" otters. Colorado was the first state to bring otters back in 1976. Other states successfully followed Colorado's lead. Now, otters can again be found in most areas of the United States.

Hardy by Nature

Otters are members of an extremely hardy family of animals known as *Mustelidae*. The mustelids include weasels, ferrets, and badgers. Weasels, and their cousins, are considered to be scrappy animals for their size, and otters are no exception.

While otters prefer playing to fighting among themselves, or with other animals, they can be ferocious

Two river otters get comfortable in the grass.

when angered. They may appear tame, but otters can be short tempered and are amazingly quick and very strong. With razor-sharp teeth and powerful jaws, otters can be quite dangerous when cornered. Determined otters have, on occasion, driven off predators as large as cougars.

Suited for the Water

North American river otters (***Lontra canadensis***) once were common across the United States. In a land of clear rivers, streams, and lakes, otters thrived on the fish that were plentiful in America's waterways. Otters are

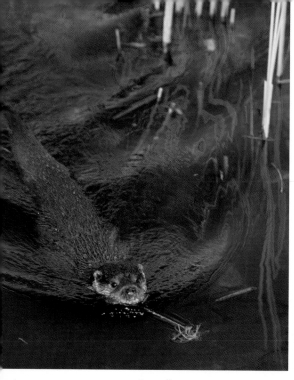

A river otter easily swims through the water by moving its tail and paws.

well suited for hunting fish and other animals that live in fresh water. About the size of a medium-size dog, otters have long, slender bodies. Adults are about three to four feet long. Full-grown otters usually weigh from fifteen to twenty-five pounds. Males generally weigh three to four pounds more than females.

In the water, otters are speedy predators. Their streamlined shape, webbed paws, and powerful tails allow otters to torpedo through the water at amazing speeds. They are the fastest-swimming freshwater mammals, reaching speeds of seven miles per hour—faster than most fish.

Otters are very good at finding their prey in the water. They have valves in their ears and noses that close tightly when they swim underwater, keeping water out. The long whiskers around their noses, called **vibrissae**, are especially sensitive to vibrations in the water made by the movement of other creatures, and help otters find food. With the aid of their whiskers, fingerlike toes, and sharp eyesight, otters have no trouble finding enough to eat.

The Fur Trade

The otter's thick fur coat, which is dark brown on top and silvery on the belly, is one of its most valuable assets, enabling it to hunt year-round. Otters actually have two fur coats that help them stay afloat and keep them warm and dry in the winter. The outer coat of long, coarse "guard hairs" helps protect the dense fur next to the otter's skin. This "underfur," with the help of waterproofing skin oils, traps air and keeps the otter dry.

Unfortunately, the otters' beautiful coats, and valuable fur, became the principal reason for their disappearance. Native peoples hunted otters long before white settlers arrived in the New World. Not until the arrival of European fur traders in the sixteenth century, however, were otters taken in large numbers. When French and English trappers came to America, they brought steel traps that were baited with food or animal scents. Curious otters were easily trapped. Because fur coats and hats were fashionable in Europe, otter pelts brought a good price.

From the beginning of the American **fur trade** in the 1500s until early in the twentieth century, otter populations were greatly reduced. From 1821 to 1891, as many as a half-million otters were killed for the fur

Gentlemen hunters spear a river otter. This was a common way of hunting otters.

trade. By 1900, otters were already extinct in some states. Yet, despite their endangered status, otters were still killed as pests in many areas well into the twentieth century.

Water Pollution

With their numbers already low because of overtrapping, other threats helped send otters toward extinction in many states. One widespread threat was poor water quality. Throughout the nineteenth century, factory production increased steadily in the United States. The waste products of manufacturing—oils, metals, and

Power plants create a lot of waste and can pollute rivers.

chemicals—were emptied into streams, rivers, and lakes. Human wastes were also dumped into the nearest water. Before the end of the century many of America's waterways were polluted.

After 1900, **fertilizers** and **pesticides** were introduced on a mass scale in American farms. The chemicals in fertilizers and pesticides were successful in increasing crops, and in killing insects and weeds. Unfortunately, many of these chemicals were washed into nearby streams and rivers whenever it rained. As a result, water quality suffered greatly, threatening fish and other animals as well.

Oils and chemicals in polluted water can harm an otter's coat by reducing its ability to trap air and keep the otter dry. In cold weather, otters are then vulnerable to **pneumonia** and other deadly infections. Also, during grooming, otters might lick the toxic oil, and die from internal bleeding.

Deposits of poisonous chemicals can also build up in the fish that live in polluted waters. When otters eat the poisoned fish they too can become sick. Sick otters may not be able to have babies, or fight diseases.

Habitat Loss

Another factor contributing to the disappearance of otters was the loss of wetlands **habitat**. Otters do best in marshy and swampy areas, which contain many of the species of prey that otters prefer.

Otters spend a great deal of time searching for food. An adult otter has to eat four times a day to keep its stomach full. Otters will eat small mammals and birds, but they prefer fish, crayfish, clams, and frogs.

On land, otters' short legs and inchworm style of running make them seem awkward. They are much faster than they appear, however. Strong legs help

An otter feasts on a crayfish.

otters move quickly. On ice and snow they can run, belly flop, and slide up to eighteen miles an hour. A fast person cannot outrun an otter.

Like all predators, otters depend on a good supply of prey to survive. When habitat is destroyed, and the otters' prey disappears, otters will move on in search of better hunting.

Historically, as America's forests and wetlands were turned into farms and towns, much of the watery habitat for otters gradually vanished. Early in the twentieth century, many swamps and marshes were drained or filled in to rid the country of disease-carrying insects. Mosquitoes, for example, breed in swamps and **marshes.** Scientists discovered that mosquitoes carry the germs responsible for infecting people with diseases like **malaria**, **yellow fever**, and **encephalitis**.

The **American Public Health Association** led a nationwide campaign to wipe out mosquitoes by eliminating wetlands. The program was successful in controlling

Otters live, breed, and play in wetlands like the one pictured.

diseases, but a great deal of wildlife habitat was gone. By the middle of the twentieth century over half of America's wetlands in the lower forty-eight states (not including Alaska and Hawaii) had been destroyed. In many areas, otters simply had no acceptable habitat left in which to live and hunt.

Hope for Otters

Otters had little chance of surviving fur trapping, water pollution, and loss of wetlands habitat. It is not surprising, therefore, that they no longer existed in many states by the 1960s. Fortunately, in a few states, such as Louisiana, otters continued to flourish (because a great deal of Louisiana is covered with water, otters have never been threatened there). Using Louisiana otters, a number of states were ready to help North American river otters make a major comeback across the country.

chapter 2

Preparing the Way

Before otters could return to the states from which they had disappeared, they needed people's help. First, otters needed protection from trapping. Then, the water in streams, rivers, and lakes had to be clean enough for otters and their prey to survive. Finally, wetlands needed to be restored so the otters could thrive in their "new" homes.

Protection for Otters

In 1826, pioneer naturalist Dr. John D. Godman predicted that, one day, otters would disappear if limits were not placed on trapping. Unfortunately, it would be another one hundred years before otters would be given any type of legal protection.

By the 1920s, it was clear that otters were becoming increasingly rare. In an attempt to prevent the few remaining otters from disappearing, states began to pass laws to restrict hunting. Indiana gave otters legal protection in 1921. Michigan began protecting them in 1925. Other states followed suit, and over the next several years, hunting seasons were established, and quotas (or limits on the number of otters that could be taken) were set. Finally, laws that made it illegal to trap otters were passed in state after state.

Eventually, states in which otters were still considered plentiful early in the twentieth century passed laws to protect them. Missouri gave otters protection in 1937. Pennsylvania did the same in 1952. When Ohio passed its first **endangered species** law in 1974, otters were listed as one of the species in trouble. Because otters remained numerous in Louisiana and a few other states, the federal government never listed the otter as endangered in its official record of species needing protection.

Cleaning Up the Water

Improving water quality was another important factor in states' efforts to successfully return otters to their natural habitat. By the middle of the twentieth century, state and national leaders were beginning to understand the harmful effects of water pollution on animals as well as humans. Outdated sewage treatment facilities, manufacturing wastes, and farm pesticides were targeted as primary sources of pollution.

Some cities voluntarily improved their sewage treatment facilities. A few manufacturers also attempted to treat their waste. But stronger action was needed. In 1948, the U.S. Congress passed the first national law aimed at cleaning up the country's water. That law, the Water Pollution Control Act, provided states with money to begin the cleanup process.

During the 1950s and 1960s, most states began cleanup programs. The goal of those programs was to reduce manufacturing and human wastes dumped into water supplies and to eliminate certain pesticides. The problem was widespread, however, and progress was extremely slow. By the 1970s, many waterways in America were still badly polluted.

In 1970, the federal government created the Environmental Protection Agency (EPA). The role of the EPA is to enforce environmental laws and eliminate pollution across the country. One of the first actions of the EPA was to ban the use of **DDT**, a toxic chemical, in pes-

Sewage treatment plants contain waste that can pollute a river otter's habitat.

ticides. DDT was known to be extremely poisonous to many species of fish. By banning DDT, fish-eating animals, like otters, were also saved.

The Clean Water Act, introduced in 1972, gave the federal government further power to force improvements in water quality. The Clean Water Act sets the standards for municipal sewage and manufacturing wastes that can be discharged into streams, rivers, and lakes. The act also gives money to city governments to pay for new and better sewage treatment facilities that would meet new treatment standards. Many treatment facilities built across the country between 1972 and

How DDT Moves Through the Food Chain

1. Humans spray DDT

2. Insects absorb pollution

3. Fish eat insects

4. Otters eat poisoned fish

1987 were funded by the Clean Water Act. By the late 1970s, many waterways were once again clean enough to support wildlife.

Restoring Habitat

For much of the twentieth century, many people believed that draining and filling in marshes and swamps were the best ways to prevent disease from mosquitoes and develop land considered useless. One group of concerned citizens in particular, however, recognized that many species of wildlife depend on wetlands for their survival.

In the 1930s, as wetlands disappeared, waterfowl hunters saw a related decline in the numbers of ducks and geese. In both the United States and Canada, those hunters convinced government leaders that wetlands should be protected. So, in 1934, the U.S. government began selling "Duck Stamps" to hunters. Since that time, the money raised through the sale of those stamps has preserved more than 5 million acres of wetlands.

Ducks Unlimited, a private conservation organization founded in 1937, has also helped protect wetlands for ducks and other animals across North America. Since its founding, Ducks Unlimited has raised over $1 billion to set aside over 9 million acres of wetlands and other wildlife habitat in the United States, Canada, and Mexico.

Unfortunately, because most people did not understand the ecological value of wetlands, many more wetlands were lost than were preserved until the 1970s. During the 1970s, scientists made people aware of the essential role that wetlands play in preventing floods, filtering pollution, and providing habitat for wildlife. The Clean Water Act of 1972 was an example of the federal government's renewed interest in saving wetlands.

Not only did the Clean Water Act help clean up water pollution, but it also became the first national wetlands law for the United States.

Additional goals for America's wetlands were set in 1987 by a panel of experts who recommended a national policy opposing the destruction of the nation's wetlands and restoring or creating new wetlands.

The struggle to save wetlands has involved private environmental organizations as well as government agencies. One of the more successful private-sector organizations has been the Nature Conservancy. A key strategy of the Nature Conservancy is to buy wetlands so that they will not be destroyed through development. To date, the Nature Conservancy has purchased more than 865,000 acres of wetlands in the United States.

Even though many wetlands were lost during the twentieth century, enough were saved that otters had sufficient habitat available to attempt reintroducing their populations.

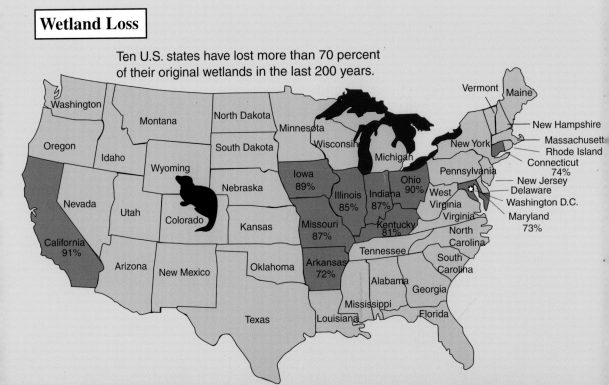

Wetland Loss

Ten U.S. states have lost more than 70 percent of their original wetlands in the last 200 years.

Washington

Montana

North Dakota

Minnesota

Vermont · Maine

New Hampshire

Oregon

Idaho

South Dakota

Wisconsin

New York

Massachusetts
Rhode Island
Connecticut
74%

Wyoming

Iowa
89%

Ohio
90%

Pennsylvania

New Jersey
Delaware
Washington D.C.
Maryland
73%

Nevada

Utah

Colorado

Nebraska

Illinois
85%

Indiana
87%

West
Virginia

Virginia

North
Carolina

California
91%

Arizona

New Mexico

Kansas

Missouri
87%

Kentucky
81%

Tennessee

South
Carolina

Oklahoma

Arkansas
72%

Alabama

Georgia

Texas

Louisiana

Mississippi

Florida

Three hikers stroll through an area that is preserved by the Nature Conservancy.

Everything in Place

Once otters were legally protected, and their watery habitat restored, the question remained—could otters be successfully reintroduced? Otters had completely disappeared from some states for many years. Indiana, for example, had had no otters for fifty years before plans were made to bring them back. Everything was in place, but until a state tried to return otters, no one knew for sure if it could be done.

chapter 3

A Remarkable Comeback

Suddenly a hush fell over the crowd that only a moment before had been buzzing with excitement. The only sound was the rushing of a cold wind through the surrounding trees. As the Indiana Fish and Wildlife trucks pulled up, the children in the crowd stood on their tiptoes to get a better look.

Out stepped two men from the Indiana Department of Natural Resources. They had just returned from the state of Louisiana, where they had collected river otters that would be set free in Indiana. The wildlife officers raised the tailgate of one of the trucks and lifted out a cage containing three squirming otters.

The cage was then carried down to the river. The clips holding it shut were cut off and the otters bounded out. They made a muttering sound, and then happily slid down to the icy water. Two of the otters dove right into the icy river and disappeared from sight. The third otter began exploring the riverbank, sniffing everything along the way.

Otters Return to Indiana

As the otters investigated their new home, the crowd cheered. It was, after all, a historic moment. Otters were back in Indiana for the first time in fifty years!

The return of river otters to the wild has been a major accomplishment. Altogether, twenty-one states have successfully restored otters to their natural habitat. What seems rather common today, however, was an

A crowd gathers to watch two river otters about to be released into the wild.

unproven idea in the mid-1970s. So, as other states watched with great interest, Colorado prepared to test the theory that the otter could thrive again.

Colorado Leads the Way

The state of Colorado decided to return river otters in 1976 in hopes of restoring an important predator to Colorado's waters. Little did the Colorado Division of Wildlife realize how far-reaching its modest **reintroduction** project would be. In the following years, the Colorado project would serve as a model for similar otter releases across the country.

River otters disappeared from Colorado's rivers and streams in 1906. Bringing them back became a priority

23

in the 1970s. The first step was to obtain the otters. Over the next several years, Colorado wildlife officials worked out wildlife trades with other locales with stable otter populations. For example, Colorado sent bighorn sheep to Oregon, elk to Newfoundland, and pine martens to Wisconsin in exchange for otters.

Between 1976 and 1991, a total of 107 otters from Oregon, Washington, Wisconsin, and Canada were returned to Colorado's waters. Those otters moved on to other areas of the state, had offspring, and their descendants survive in Colorado today.

Missouri's Grand Plan

Popular support for bringing otters back to Missouri grew in the 1970s. An important first step took place in 1976, when Missouri established the nation's first conservation sales tax. Taxpayers would pay for otters to be returned, and for other wildlife programs, with the monies raised. Thereafter, an ambitious plan was developed to restore otters into every river system in the state.

The Missouri Department of Conservation began the state's otter reintroduction project in 1982 with a three-way trade of animals among Missouri, Kentucky, and Louisiana. Missouri's part of the agreement was to send thirty-two wild turkeys to Kentucky. Kentucky, in return, hired trappers in Louisiana to capture twenty otters that were then shipped to Missouri.

After the first successful release, several more releases were scheduled over the next few years. These otters reproduced so successfully that the Missouri Department of Conservation estimates that from eleven thousand to eighteen thousand otters now live in Missouri. Without question, Missouri's otter program has been the most successful program of its kind in North America.

An otter is weighed before being released back to its natural habitat.

Community Support in New York

Otters never completely disappeared from the Adirondack Mountains region of eastern New York State. But by the 1960s, otters were gone from all other regions of New York. The challenge, therefore, was to live-trap otters in the eastern part of New York and release them elsewhere in the state.

A special partnership was formed to raise money for the otter project. People of widely different back-grounds, including trappers, **conservationists**, educa-tors, business leaders, wildlife **rehabilitators**, and Wildlife Department officials, joined the partnership. The success of their efforts shows that people can work together for a common goal. A total of 279 otters have

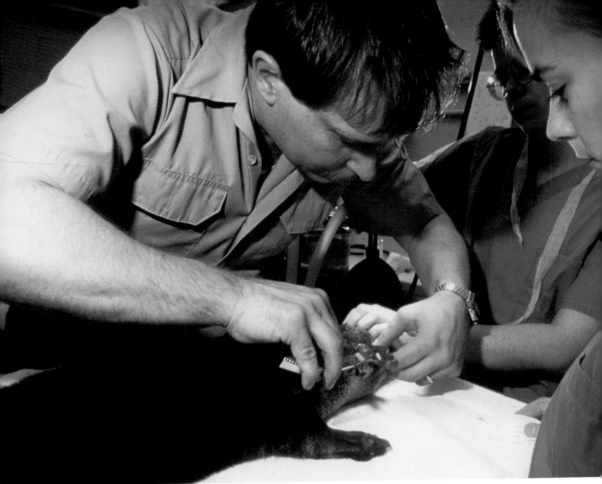

Conservationists tag an otter's ear so they can identify it later.

now been released in the nine sites selected for the release project.

The New York River Otter Project also includes schoolchildren as important fund-raisers. And children have been present at all otter releases in New York. Students from the Rochester School for the Deaf were even allowed to turn the otters loose.

Louisiana Otters

A number of states have contributed otters for reintroduction projects, but most of the otters have come from Louisiana. One family from Theriot, Louisiana, has supplied the majority of the otters that have been shipped from Louisiana to other states. Diane and Lee Roy Sevin own the Bayou Otter Farm, and many wildlife officials refer to them as the "godparents of otter reintroductions." The Sevins buy otters from local trappers and keep the pregnant females until they give birth to their pups. After giving birth, the adult otters are returned to the swamps, and the Sevins raise the pups for the reintroduction projects. They have supplied more than twenty-four hundred otters to states across the country.

In Louisiana, and other states, private trappers have been hired to live-trap otters for shipment to other areas. Without the help of trappers, otters would not be back in many states today.

Two river otters peek through the bushes to explore their surroundings.

Otters Return to State After State

Through the cooperation of individuals, private organizations, and governmental agencies, otters have now been returned to twenty-one states: Arizona, Colorado, Illinois, Indiana, Iowa, Kansas, Kentucky, Maryland, Minnesota, Missouri, Nebraska, New York, North Carolina, Ohio, Oklahoma, Pennsylvania, Tennessee, Texas, Utah, Virginia, and West Virginia.

An excited river otter scurries into the water as people photograph its release.

The Return of River Otters

River otters have been returned to twenty-one states.

■ Returned River Otters

The reintroduction of river otters across the United States has been one of the most successful and exciting wildlife comebacks in recent times. It appears that in almost every state where an effort has been made to return otters, they have settled into their new homes, given birth to pups, and spread out into new territories. The only question that remains is whether otters can survive into the future.

chapter 4

The Future for Otters

It is early spring and Scott Johnson of the Indiana Department of Natural Resources has traveled to the site of Indiana's first otter release at Muscatatuck National Wildlife Refuge in Seymour. He has come to see how the otters are doing. Before they were released into the wild, the first otters were fitted with tiny radio transmitters. The transmitters send out signals that Scott can pick up with his radio receiving equipment. He follows the signals in an effort to find the den of a female otter. When a female limits her activity in the spring, it's a sign that she may be making a den to have pups (also called cubs).

Tracking an Otter

Scott follows the beeps, which get louder as he gets closer to the female he is tracking. Finally, he locates a den that would have been almost impossible to find without the radio signals. When he takes a closer look, he sees what appears to be a very small otter tail. He creeps closer until he can peek into the den. It takes a few seconds for his eyes to grow accustomed to the darkness inside . . . and then he sees the eyes of a tiny otter pup staring back at him.

Scott quietly backs away. He does not want to disturb the pup or agitate the pup's mother. Once safely out of range, Scott stops to think about what he has just seen. All the months of planning and preparation, and all the hard work by so many people, have paid off— otters are, once again, raising families in Indiana.

If otters are to survive where they have been reintroduced, they will have to breed and successfully raise young. Most otters remain alone throughout the year, and only come together during breeding season. Breeding usually occurs from December through April. Male and female otters use the scent glands located near their tails to mark tufts of grass or mounds of leaves and mud. That allows them to find each other during the breeding season.

A litter of one to six, but usually two to three, pups is born in late winter or early spring. Otter pups are generally between four and nine inches long. They are

An otter and her pup (right) pause on the river rocks to sniff the air.

toothless and their eyes are shut. The mother raises the helpless pups by herself, until they are about five to six months old and able to get around on their own. At that point, the father may rejoin the family, and they will hunt and play together. The pups will stay with their parents until they are almost a year old. Then they will go off on their own, although they do not always go very far away.

Two years after birth, otters are old enough to breed and have babies of their own. They find mates and the cycle starts all over again.

Threats Remain

There can be little doubt that river otters have made a strong comeback, but can they continue to survive into the future? While they seem to be heading in the right direction, a number of threats still remain. Though a single threat would not by itself eliminate the otter, the combination of several threats could have a devastating effect.

Reintroduced otters have returned to areas that are now criss-crossed by roads carrying much heavier traffic than fifty years ago. Wherever we find otters today, we know that one of the primary reasons they die is because they are hit by cars and trucks.

Most states that have brought otters back still maintain strict laws against the trapping of otters. Trapping of other animals that are not considered endangered, however, is still allowed. Beavers, for example, are legally trapped for their fur. Unfortunately, beavers and otters share the same habitat, and sometimes otters are accidentally caught in beaver traps.

Water quality has improved quite a bit, but pollution has not been eliminated completely. If people really want otters to survive, they need to support efforts to

An otter's paw is stuck in the jaws of a steel trap.

eliminate pollution from streams, rivers, and lakes. Without strong law enforcement, water pollution could become a serious problem for otters once again.

A growing number of groups have been successful in restoring wetland habitats for waterfowl and animals like otters. Because of their efforts, many wetlands have been saved. But marshes and swamps are still disappearing. Ohio, for example, continues to lose wetlands at an alarming rate despite efforts to save them.

Two river otters take a stroll along ice-covered water on the
Tippecanoe River in Indiana.

Today, the primary threat to wetlands is human
development. Every day, throughout America, wetlands
are being turned into housing developments, industrial
parks, shopping centers, golf courses, and farms. As long
as people continue to convert wildlife habitat into
places to live, work, and play, all animals, not just otters,
will be threatened.

Reducing Otter/People Conflict

One of the greatest challenges to maintaining healthy
populations of otters is to minimize conflict between
otters and people.

As otters increase in numbers and spread out into
new territories, their taste for fish and skill as predators
put them in direct competition with fishermen. When it
was announced that otters would be reintroduced into
Great Smoky Mountain National Park in Tennessee, for
example, some fishermen threatened to shoot them.

Scientific studies of otters' fishing patterns have yielded mixed results. In Tennessee, studies found that fishermen have little reason to complain. Otters will occasionally take popular game fish like trout, bass,

A hungry otter enjoys the taste of a fish it has just caught.

A woman hopes to catch fish as she casts her line into a cool stream.

perch, salmon, and pike. But they normally take slower-moving fish that feed on river bottoms like carp, suckers, and mudminnows. Most fishermen do not prefer those fish. In fact, it is more likely that otters actually help increase the numbers of "sport" fish by eliminating fish that compete with them for food.

A study of the eating habits of otters in Missouri, however, shows that otters eat "sport fish" more often than other fish. Those fish include largemouth bass, smallmouth bass, rock bass, and longear sunfish.

Otters have also become a problem for people who raise fish for a living. In some cases, otters have raided large amounts of fish from fish hatcheries. One possible solution for this problem is for state wildlife agencies to restock fishponds that have been raided by otters.

Ongoing Success Story

On the whole, reaction to the reintroduction of otters to the nation's waterways is very positive. A great number of people, in many different parts of the country, have worked very hard to reintroduce otters. Across America, a total of twenty-one states have successfully

A family of otters basks in the sun on a riverbank.

returned over four thousand otters. Otters can be found in forty-seven states, and their numbers appear to be growing steadily.

This is, unquestionably one of the most successful predator restoration projects ever attempted in North America. The reintroduction of otters can now be used as a model for the reintroduction of other species that are near extinction. And hopefully, people who understand the importance of otters will work to make sure that they stay around forever.

American Public Health Association: An organization of public health professionals dedicated to preventing diseases and promoting health.

conservationist: A person who supports the conservation of natural resources.

DDT: A toxic chemical compound, formerly widely used as a pesticide.

encephalitis: A serious illness spread by mosquitoes, and characterized by high fever, stiff neck, and swelling of the brain.

endangered species: A type of plant or animal that is nearing extinction.

extinction: The complete and permanent elimination of a plant or animal species.

fertilizer: Any substance used to enrich the soil with nutrients, especially a commercial or chemical manure.

fur trade: The business of buying and selling animal skins.

habitat: The locality or living space of a plant or animal.

Lontra canadensis: The scientific name for the North American river otter.

malaria: A group of serious diseases carried by mosquitoes, and characterized by attacks of chills, fever, and sweating.

marsh: A shallow wetland dominated by cattails, reeds, and similar types of nonwoody plants.

Mustelidae: A family of animals that includes badgers, minks, otters, skunks, and wolverines.

pesticide: A chemical preparation for destroying plant, fungus, or animal pests.

pneumonia: A severe infection of the lungs caused by a harmful bacteria.

rehabilitator: A person who helps restore the ill or injured to a condition of good health.

reintroduction: Introducing again, as in returning animals to areas from which they disappeared.

vibrissae: Stiff, coarse hairs richly supplied with nerves, found especially around the nose, and with a sensory function.

wetlands: Land that has a wet and spongy soil, as a marsh, swamp, or bog.

wildlife: Undomesticated animals living in the wild.

yellow fever: An acute, infectious disease of warm climates, caused by a virus transmitted by a mosquito.

Books

M. Barbara Brownell, *Amazing Otters*. Washington, DC: National Geographic Society, 1990. Describes the habitat and physical characteristics of sea otters and river otters.

Barbara Juster Esbensen, *Playful Slider: The North American Otter.* Boston: Little, Brown, 1993. Rich illustrations enhance this examination of how otters live, hunt, and play year-round.

Ewan McLeish, *Keeping Water Clean*. Austin, TX: Raintree Steck-Vaughn, 1998. A look at how water becomes polluted, the worldwide problems associated with the issue, and ways that people can eliminate pollution.

Sandy Ransford, *The Otter.* New York: Kingfisher, 1999. The story of otters: how they hunt, find mates, build their homes, and raise their young.

April Pulley Sayre, *Wetland*. New York: Twenty-First Century Books, 1996. A book devoted to describing the role of wetland habitats in the balance of nature.

Frank Staub, *America's Wetlands*. Minneapolis: Carolrhoda Books, 1995. A guide to the full range of wetlands found across America and their role in the ecosystem.

Darlene R. Stille, *Water Pollution.* Chicago: Childrens Press, 1990. A simple yet informative book that explains the importance of water, causes of pollution, and ways to clean up polluted water.

Darlene R. Stille, *Wetlands*. Chicago: Childrens Press, 1999. A basic examination of the variety of water systems included under the term "wetlands" and their importance to plant and animal life.

Organizations to Contact

Ducks Unlimited, Inc.
One Waterfowl Way
Memphis, TN 38102
(901) 758-3825
website: www.ducks.org

Environmental Protection Agency (EPA)
Office of Wetlands, Oceans, and Watersheds
401 M St. SW
Washington, DC 20460
(800) 832-7828
website: www.epa.gov/owow

International Otter Survival Fund
Skye Environmental Centre, Ltd.
Broadford
Isle of Skye IV49 9AQ
++44 (1471) 822 487
website: www.otter.org

The Nature Conservancy
4245 N. Fairfax Dr., Suite 100
Arlington, VA 22203
(703) 841-5300
website: www.tnc.org

Otternet
website: www.otternet.com

Acknowledgments

Jan Reed-Smith, John Ball Zoo

Scott Johnson, Indiana Department of Natural Resources

Greg Linscombe, Louisiana Department of Wildlife & Fisheries

Denis Case and Gary Hoskins, Ohio Department of Natural Resources

David Hamilton, Missouri Department of Conservation

Tom Beck, Colorado Division of Wildlife

Bruce Penrod, New York State Department of Environmental Conservation

Dennis Money, New York River Otter Project

Lee Roy and Diane Sevin, Bayou Otter Farm

Carrie Gluck, American Public Health Association

Lisa Maloney, Worthington Estates Elementary School

Shay Baker, Arts and Science Links

Dr. John E. Becker writes children's books and magazine articles about nature and wild animals. He graduated from Ohio State University in the field of education. He has been an elementary school teacher, college professor, zoo administrator, and has worked in the field of wildlife conservation with the International Society for Endangered Cats. He currently lives in Delaware, Ohio, and teaches writing at the Thurber Writing Academy. He also enjoys visiting schools and sharing his love of writing with kids. In his spare time, Dr. Becker likes to read, hike in the woods, ice skate, and play tennis.